HOW DO GARDEN GROW?

by Mirabella Mendez
illustrated by Pearl Beach

Harcourt

Orlando   Boston   Dallas   Chicago   San Diego

Visit *The Learning Site!*

www.harcourtschool.com

Let's grow a garden! We can plant some seeds. We can watch them grow!

Let's dig up the dirt. We can use
shovels to turn over the dirt.

Let's plant lots of seeds. The seeds
are different shapes. The seeds are
different sizes.

Some seeds will grow into
vegetables. Some seeds will grow
into flowers. Some seeds won't
grow at all.

Let's plant lots of flowers. Flowers
will look beautiful. Flowers will smell
wonderful.

Let's plant lots of vegetables. We can plant lettuce, beans, and peppers. We can plant carrots, tomatoes, and beets.

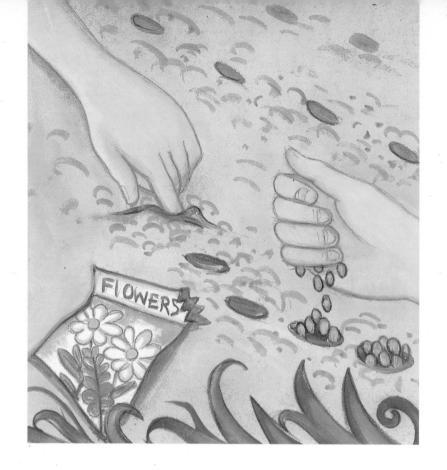

Let's make holes in the ground. Plop!
We drop the seeds into the holes.
Then we cover the seeds with dirt.

Seeds need sunlight and water to grow. Let's water the garden everyday. The sun will warm the seeds.

The seeds sprout into green shoots!
The shoots stick up in the dirt. The
shoots grow into plants.

Let's check the garden. The plants are growing fast! The flowers are starting to bloom.

Let's look at the tomatoes. The plants are very tall. The tomatoes are still small. When will we be able to eat them?

Let's look at the things that live in the garden. Bees buzz on the flowers. Butterflies land on the leaves. An earthworm crawls in the dirt.

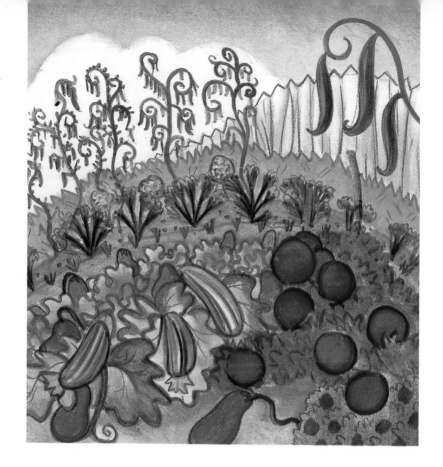

Let's check the vegetables in the garden. Here are tomatoes and squash! Here are beans and peas! Here are carrots and radishes!

Let's check the flowers in the garden.
Here is a sunflower as tall as a
person! Here is a rose that smells
sweet.

Let's pick the flowers. Let's eat the juicy red tomatoes. Let's make a salad. We grew a wonderful garden!